MT. PLEAS
MT. PLEASANT, IOWA

GETTING TO KNOW OUR PLANET
GREAT BARRIER REEF
BY VICKY FRANCHINO

Published in the United States of America by Cherry Lake Publishing
Ann Arbor, Michigan
www.cherrylakepublishing.com

Content Adviser: Linda Hooper-Bùi, PhD, Associate Professor, Department of
Environmental Science, Louisiana State University Agricultural Center, Baton Rouge, Louisiana
Reading Adviser: Marla Conn, Read With Me Now

Photo Credits: Cover and page 1, © Debra James/Shutterstock.com; page 5 and 7,
© Pete Niesen/Shutterstock.com; page 9, © Ethan Daniels/Shutterstock.com; page 11,
© melissaf84/Shutterstock.com; page 13, © imageBROKER/Alamy Stock Photo; page 15,
© kaschibo/Shutterstock.com; page 17, © Birdiegal/Shutterstock.com; page 19, © Ozimages/
Alamy Stock Photo; page 21, © frantisekhojdysz/Shutterstock.com.

LIBRARY OF CONGRESS CATALOGING-IN-PUBLICATION DATA
Library of Congress Cataloging-in-Publication data on file.

Cherry Lake Publishing would like to acknowledge the
work of The Partnership for 21st Century Skills. Please
visit *www.p21.org* for more information.

Printed in the United States of America
Corporate Graphics
January 2016

GREAT BARRIER REEF

CONTENTS

GETTING TO KNOW OUR PLANET

UNDERWATER CITY

Look into the waters off the northeastern coast of Australia. You'll see a magical place! There are plants, fish, and sea creatures of all sizes. This is the Great Barrier Reef. It is a huge structure. In fact, it's more than 1,250 miles (2,012 kilometers) long. Astronauts can see the reef from outer space!

Bright orange soldierfish swim in the Great Barrier Reef.

Some people call coral reefs the "rain forests of the ocean." Both ecosystems are filled with many different living things. What do you know about the Great Barrier Reef? What questions do you have about it?

5

A reef is a **ridge** near the ocean's surface. Many reefs are made of rock or sand. The Great Barrier Reef is made of coral. Coral is hard. It may look like a type of rock, but it isn't. It is actually the skeleton of a living creature!

The Great Barrier Reef is easy to spot from above.

Most coral reefs are in fairly shallow water. This is because coral feeds on a plant called algae. Most algae need sunlight to grow. There is more sunlight near the water's surface. What might happen to coral in deeper water?

7

BUILDING BLOCKS

The Great Barrier Reef is made of millions of coral **polyps**. A coral looks like a tiny tube. One side attaches to a hard surface. The other has long limbs called tentacles to collect food. Many corals join together and create a **colony**. Each coral makes a hard outer skeleton. When the coral dies, this skeleton is left behind. New coral polyps attach themselves to it.

A coral polyp has many small tentacles.

LOOK!

Certain rocks are also made of living things. Sedimentary rocks form from layers of soil and plants. They harden over millions of years. Look for rocks that have layers near your home or school. These rocks might be sedimentary!

9

Coral is very small. As a result, reefs grow slowly. Some grow only 1 inch (2.5 centimeters) each year! The Great Barrier Reef formed over hundreds of thousands of years. About 400 different kinds of coral are in this reef. Look at the amazing colors and shapes they create!

Different types of coral can look very different from one another.

THINK!

When corals are alive and eating algae, they're colorful. When a coral dies, it turns white. Why do you think this might be?

11

SEA CREATURES

Many different animals live in the Great Barrier Reef. There are thousands of **species** of fish. They come in a range of sizes and colors. Whales, crocodiles, dolphins, manatees, and turtles also live there. One interesting reef animal is the dugong. This animal spends its life swimming in the ocean. But it looks a bit like its land relative, the elephant!

12

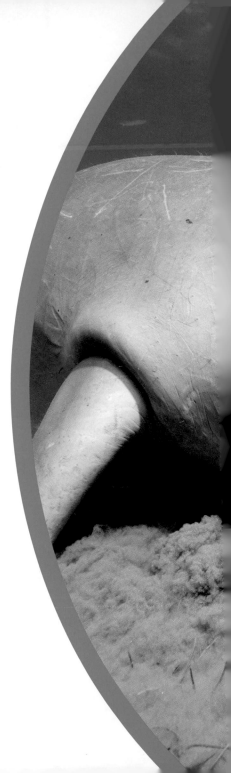

A dugong munches on seaweed near the Great Barrier Reef.

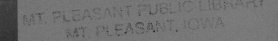

MAKE A GUESS!

Some sea turtle species visit the Great Barrier Reef to lay eggs. Why is the reef a good place to do this? Make a guess. Then check your answer online or in a book. Were you right?

13

Many animals of the Great Barrier Reef are dangerous. Watch out for the blue-ringed octopus. It might look harmless. However, its bite can kill a person in minutes. Jellyfish have a painful sting. Also, be on the lookout for the cone shell's poisonous dart! The great white shark has rows of scary-looking teeth. It's usually a bigger threat to fish than to humans.

A blue-ringed octopus's rings show up when it's scared or angry.

The crown-of-thorns starfish feeds on coral. This damages the Great Barrier Reef. Some people argue that we should get rid of this starfish. Others say we shouldn't. What do you think? What good things might happen after changing an ecosystem? What bad things?

Not all wildlife lives underwater at the Great Barrier Reef. Some wildlife lives on the surface. More than 200 different kinds of birds are found there. Some live on the Great Barrier Reef all year. Others visit during their **migration**. All these birds like the area's warm temperatures. They can easily find good things to eat.

Some sooty terns lay their eggs at the Great Barrier Reef.

Algae plants are extremely important. They are food for coral. They also act like a special "glue" to help a coral reef grow. This glue attracts more life that clings to the reef. This makes the reef larger. Do you live near bodies of water? Have you seen algae in a lake, river, or stream?

PEOPLE AND THE GREAT BARRIER REEF

Some **native** groups have long lived on and near the Great Barrier Reef for thousands of years. The Aboriginal and Torres Strait Islander peoples rely on this reef. They use it for food and shelter. They also travel along the reef in their boats. Many of their traditions are closely tied to the reef.

Many native islanders still live on the Torres Strait Islands.

THINK!

The Great Barrier Reef is easy to damage. A changing climate, **pollution**, and too much fishing cause major problems. Even too much sunscreen from swimmers can upset the ecosystem! How can people protect the reef?

Millions of people visit the Great Barrier Reef each year. It is exciting to see the local animals and plants. The government of Australia is working hard to protect this reef. Would you like to visit the Great Barrier Reef? What might be the best things to see or do?

A diver watches a blue-spotted stingray swim through the reef.

CREATE!

Make a piece of art to celebrate this amazing place! You could use paper, paint, crayons, clay, or other materials. Use your imagination! Be sure to include lots of colors. The Great Barrier Reef is a natural rainbow!

21

GLOSSARY

colony (KAH-luh-nee) a large group of animals that live together

ecosystems (EE-koh-sis-tuhmz) the living things in places and their relationship to their environments

migration (mye-GRAY-shun) the act of moving to another area or climate at a specific time of year

native (NAY-tiv) a person who was born in or lives in a particular place

pollution (puh-LOO-shuhn) harmful materials that damage the air, water, and soil

polyps (PAH-luhps) small sea animals with a tubelike body and tentacles

ridge (RIJ) a narrow, raised strip of rock, stone, or sand

species (SPEE-sheez) one of the groups into which living things are divided; members of the same species can mate and have offspring

FIND OUT MORE

BOOKS

Banting, Erinn. *Great Barrier Reef*. North Mankato, MN: AV2 by Weigl, 2013.

Woolf, Alex. *Sailing the Great Barrier Reef*. New York: Gareth Stevens, 2015.

WEB SITES

Kids Discover—Spotlight: Coral Reefs
www.kidsdiscover.com/spotlight/coral-reefs
Look at pictures and learn some fun facts about the Great Barrier Reef.

National Geographic—Great Barrier Reef
*http://video.nationalgeographic.com/video/oceans-narrated-by
-sylvia-earle/oceans-barrier-reef*
This video from National Geographic shows just how beautiful the Great Barrier Reef is!

INDEX

24

ABOUT THE AUTHOR

Vicky Franchino enjoys learning new things and has written many books about interesting places, people, and animals. She would like to see some of the 400 types of coral at the Great Barrier Reef—especially the ones that look like trees and brains!—as well as the fish. Aren't they beautiful? Vicky lives with her family in Wisconsin and would be willing to go on the very (very!) long plane ride that a trip to the reef would require!